STAR SIGNS
FOR KIDS

Nicky Bentley

For Bree
who defies the stars
by reaching for them

INTRODUCTION

Do you know your star sign? Perhaps you've already looked at what it said about you. Did you agree? Astrology isn't about who you are, but where you fit into the universe.

Astrology is the study of how celestial objects (things like planets, stars and moons) affects human lives. Astrologists believe that every single person is deeply connected to the rest of the universe. The time and place you were born—down to the exact second—helps to figure out what influence* your star sign has on your personality. If you think about it, nobody was born in exactly the same place and time as you. Not even your twin—if you have one!

Being born under the same star sign doesn't make people the same as one another. When people lead different lives, they get different ideas and interests, but if you were born under the same star sign (sometimes called sun signs), you'll face similar challenges.

On the next page is a description of all the things you're going to find out about your star sign.

* to influence is to have an effect on behaviour

STAR SIGN

how it is pronounced

Day and month of your birthday

Symbol: This is what represents your sign.

Star Gem: Not the same as your birthstone.

Element: Fire, Earth, Air or Water

Colour: The colour that has the strongest effect on you.

Ruler: The planet, star or moon that rules your emotions.

House: The zodiac is divided into twelve houses, like a clock.

Best At: What your star sign is best known for.

Friends: The star signs you are more likely to connect with.

Likes and Dislikes: What triggers you the most.

Personality: Not many people will have <u>every</u> trait, so use the positive and negative traits as a guide.

ARIES

pronounced: AIR-reez

March 21 — April 19

Symbol: The Ram
Element: Fire
Ruler: Mars
House of Self
Likes: Being active

Star Gem: Diamond
Colour: Red
Friends: Leo, Sagittarius
Best At: Motivating
Dislikes: Delays

Personality

Arians love adventure but can also be reckless and impulsive (they rush into things). With bundles of energy and courage, Aries is ambitious, wanting to do, be and have everything, and will work to get it. They are pioneers—the first to discover new things. Quick-acting, Aries can also be quick-to-anger, but they don't hold a grudge. They are confident and passionate (they have strong opinions about all sorts of things). This can also make them an enthusiastic kind of person, but also impatient, because they don't want to wait!

TAURUS

pronounced: TOUR-iss

April 20 — May 20

Symbol: The Bull
Element: Earth
Ruler: Venus
House of Worth
Likes: Creating

Star Gem: Emerald
Colour: Green
Friends: Virgo, Capricorn
Best At: Teaching
Dislikes: Complications

Personality

Taureans are loyal and dependable—the type of person who supports friends and family even when the going gets tough. They are creative and appreciate art and surrounding beauty, but can be materialistic (wanting lots of things and money) and greedy—caring too much about their luxuries and getting possessive. The Taurus has a warm heart and loads of patience, which means they make good leaders. While they can be stubborn, they also have loads of determination—which means they always reach their goal.

GEMINI

pronounced: JEM-in-eye

May 21 — June 20

Symbol: The Twins
Element: Air
Ruler: Mercury
House of Communication
Likes: Going out

Star Gem: Pearl
Colour: Yellow
Friends: Libra, Aquarius
Best At: Multi-tasking
Dislikes: Routine

Personality

Geminis are a social sign and are eloquent—(they can express themselves clearly). Adaptable, the Gemini won't have problems with change, except when they change their minds too much, making them indecisive and inconsistent. When this happens, they can become nervous and tense. Intelligent and charming, they are a talkative sign, but at times don't listen enough. They are curious, fascinated and inspired by the world around them, which makes them great travel buddies.

CANCER

pronounced: KAN-sir

June 21 — July 22

Symbol: The Crab
Element: Water
Ruler: The Moon
House: Security
Likes: Hobbies at home

Star Gem: Ruby
Colour: White
Friends: Scorpio, Pisces
Best At: Helping
Dislikes: Strangers

Personality

Emotional and loving, Cancers have deep souls. They are intuitive (they rely on how they feel more than logic). They are cautious, making them harder to get to know, but once accepted, a Cancer is a loyal friend. Their strong emotions can also make them insecure and over-sensitive, becoming clingy with the ones they love. They are imaginative, which sometimes ends in pessimism (when they imagine the worst). If someone does end up needing their help, they are generous and nurturing.

LEO

pronounced: LEE-oh

July 23 – August 22

Symbol: The Lion
Element: Fire
Ruler: The Sun
House: Pleasure
Likes: Drama

Star Gem: Peridot
Colour: Gold
Friends: Sagittarius, Aries
Best At: Leading
Dislikes: Being ignored

Personality

Leos are charismatic (people find them charming) and dignified. Because of this, and the fact they are fearless, they are natural leaders. Sometimes they can be arrogant—(they think they are the best) and patronising (they believe they know what's best for everyone else). They can also bring people together and have fun, as they are cheerful and generous. If they are not controlling the event, they can become inflexible (they don't want anything to change and won't even talk about it) but their love of laughter and warm spirit will win the day.

VIRGO

pronounced: VER-go

Aug 23 – Sep 22

Symbol: The Virgin
Element: Earth
Ruler: Mercury
House: Routine
Likes: Books

Star Gem: Sapphire
Colour: Brown
Friends: Capricorn, Taurus
Best At: Planning
Dislikes: Asking for help

Personality

The Virgo is known to be practical and intelligent. They have attention to detail but can also be perfectionists, never happy with their results. This also leads to them being picky and critical of others. Virgos are hardworking and organised. They are analytical (they use logic and order)— and are great problem solvers. They are modest about their success and getting attention isn't important to them. They enjoy material wealth (owning lots of things), but can be fussy if the quality isn't the very best.

LIBRA

pronounced: LIB-ruh or LEE-bra

Sep 23 — Oct 22

Symbol: The Scales
Element: Air
Ruler: Venus
House: Relationships
Likes: Sharing

Star Gem: Opal
Colour: Pink
Friends: Gemini, Aquarius
Best At: Judging
Dislikes: Conflict

Personality

Known for being friendly and charming, Libra is fair-minded and has a strong sense of harmony and justice. They are diplomatic (careful not to hurt anyone's feelings) and try to find the most balanced result. Sometimes this makes them indecisive. A social sign, Librans do not like being alone. Because of their trusting nature, they can be gullible (they believe anything) and easily-influenced (letting others guide them). They can also be rather self-indulgent (doing only what they want) and rely on others to inspire them into action. They are fantastic team-players.

SCORPIO

pronounced: SKOR-pee-oh

Oct 23 — Nov 21

Symbol: The Scorpion
Element: Water
Ruler: Pluto & Mars
House: Transformation
Likes: Being right

Star Gem: Citrine
Colour: Black
Friends: Pisces, Cancer
Best At: Keeping Secrets
Dislikes: Dishonesty

Personality

Scorpios are a passionate sign, having intense emotions and reactions to whatever they come across. This makes them exciting to people around them. They are also curious, wanting to know everything about everyone. Perhaps this is why they are secretive, not wanting others to know too much about them. When something captures their attention, they can be obsessive (it's always on their mind). If they don't get what they want, they can be jealous or resentful (feeling bitter towards someone or something). Their determination and bravery makes them a powerful friend.

SAGITTARIUS

pronounced: sa-ji-TAIR-ree-iss

Nov 22 – Dec 21

Symbol: The Archer
Element: Fire
Planet: Jupiter
House: Expansion
Likes: Travel

Star Gem: Topaz
Colour: Purple
Friends: Leo, Aries
Best At: Learning
Dislikes: Details

Personality

Idealistic and optimistic (they always see the positive side), the Sagittarian is happy and carefree. They are very honest, but their honesty can be too blunt, harsh and tactless. While they are intelligent and philosophical, they can become argumentative, because they are confident they are right. They love their freedom, to the point where they can be irresponsible (avoiding their duties). They are an active sign, and love being outdoors.

CAPRICORN
pronounced: KAP-ri-korn

Dec 22 – Jan 19

Symbol: The Sea-Goat
Element: Earth
Planet: Saturn
House: Career
Likes: Tradition

Star Gem: Garnet
Colour: Grey
Friends: Taurus, Virgo
Best At: Providing
Dislikes: Chaos

Personality

Capricorns are hard-working and ambitious (they have a strong desire to succeed). They are practical and disciplined (working with focus and order) to achieve their goal. They are known to be responsible, but can also be unforgiving and rigid. They can be pessimistic and miserly (hoarding wealth and spending as little as possible). In spite of this, they are wonderful providers for their loved ones, and take on the role of protector in the family.

AQUARIUS
pronounced: ah-KWAIR-ree-iss

Jan 20 — Feb 18

Symbol: The Water-Bearer
Element: Air
Planet: Uranus
House: Community
Likes: Helping others

Star Gem: Amethyst
Colour: Blue
Friends: Libra, Gemini
Best At: Listening
Dislikes: Being bored

Personality

Aquarians are unpredictable and exciting, who love to be challenged. Inventive and intellectual, their ideas go in many different directions—but they can be uncompromising (unwilling to work with other people's ideas). They are compassionate and humanitarian (wanting to make the world a better place for all humans). If they feel restricted, they will be temperamental until they have the freedom to roam again. They are independent but can also be aloof (cool and distant). Aquarians are known to be honest and loyal.

PISCES

pronounced: PIE-seez

Feb 19 — Mar 20

Symbol: The Fishes
Element: Water
Planet: Neptune
House: Subconscious
Likes: Being alone

Star Gem: Aquamarine
Colour: Light Green
Friends: Cancer, Scorpio
Best At: Spirituality
Dislikes: Criticism

Personality

Pisceans are intuitive and ruled by their feelings. They are creative and imaginative, lost in a world of their own making... and can be escapist (to refuse to face something unpleasant). They tend to be passive, not choosing their path but going with the flow. Because they are kind and forgiving, they can be friends with very different people. Their selfless but weak-willed nature makes them easy to manipulate. They can be amazing in the arts but too shy and secretive to show their talent. They are the most sensitive starsign.

EXTRA INFORMATION

Fire signs have enthusiasm, courage and are inspiring.
Earth signs are strong, determined and focused.
Air signs are social, honest and have sharp minds.
Water signs are sensitive, nurturing and intuitive.

The Zodiac: The twelve star signs together is called the zodiac. The zodiac is usually pictured as a wheel.

Born on the cusp: If you are born on the very first or very last day of your star sign, you can feel the influence of the star sign you just missed out on.

Horoscope: Predictions made every day, week, month or year about what might affect your regular life.

Cardinal Signs: Aries, Cancer, Libra and Capricorn.
These signs start the season and have initiative.

Fixed Signs: Taurus, Leo, Scorpio and Aquarius.
These signs carry the weight of each season, and are strong.

Mutable Signs: Gemini, Virgo, Sagittarius and Pisces
These signs finish the season and embrace change.

CHINESE ASTROLOGY

Were you born in January or February? Chinese New Year moves between January 21 and February 20 — so your Chinese zodiac sign might not be obvious!

Year of the Rat: 2008, 1996, 1984, 1972, 1960
The rat represents wisdom.
Charming, timid, practical, greedy and social

Year of the Ox: 2009, 1997, 1985, 1973, 1961
The ox is industrious, meaning hard-working.
Honest, stubborn, creative, lazy and patient.

Year of the Tiger: 2010, 1998, 1986, 1974, 1962
The trait of this sign is valour—meaning bravery.
Friendly, reckless, charming, boastful and confident.

Year of the Rabbit: 2011, 1999, 1987, 1975, 1963
The trait of this sign is caution.
Kind, secretive, friendly, superficial and gentle.

Year of the Dragon: 2012, 2000, 1988, 1976, 1964
The dragon represents strength.
Successful, arrogant, clever, hot-headed and kind.

Year of the Snake: 2013, 2001, 1989, 1977, 1965
The snake represents passiveness.
Respectful, greedy, sympathetic, vain and agile.

Year of the Horse: 2014, 2002, 1990, 1978, 1966
The horse represents forging ahead—enthusiasm.
Active, selfish, witty, over-confident and persuasive.

Year of the Ram/Goat: 2015, 2003, 1991, 1979, 1967
The ram or goat represents unity.
Polite, unrealistic, imaginative wilful and determined.

Year of the Monkey: 2016, 2004, 1992, 1980, 1968
The trait of the monkey is flexibility.
Cheerful, snobby, inventive, restless and energetic.

Year of the Rooster: 2017, 2005, 1993, 1981, 1969
The rooster is punctual and reliable.
Neat, arrogant, independent, materialistic and kind.

Year of the Dog: 2018, 2006, 1994, 1982, 1970
The dog represents loyalty.
Honest, stubborn, friendly, critical and smart.

Year of the Pig: 2019, 2007, 1995, 1983, 1971
The trait of the pig is amiability.
Carefree, gullible, trusting, sincere and hot-headed.

CPSIA information can be obtained
at www.ICGtesting.com
Printed in the USA
BVHW021541260321
603339BV00015B/1008